AROUND THE WORLD

FRANCE

First published in 1997 in the USA by
Thunder Bay Press
5880 Oberlin Drive, Suite 400
San Diego, CA 92121

ISBN 1 57145 084 X

Library of Congress Cataloging-in-Publication Data available upon request

Editions of this book will appear simultaneously
in France, Germany, Great Britain, Italy, Spain
and Holland under the auspices of
Euredition bv, Den Haag, Netherlands

Translated from the French by Marjolijn de Jager
Typesetting: Buro AD, Amersfoort
Printed by AUBIN IMPRIMEUR, Poitiers, France

Around the World

FRANCE

Noël Graveline

THUNDER BAY
P·R·E·S·S

INTRODUCTION

Discovering France means, in the first place, approaching a geography shaped like a mosaic rather than a hexagon. Even though the country is bordered by three bodies of water and an equal number of harmoniously distributed continental land parts, that is not sufficient reason to lock it into a simple geometric figure. Similarly, if one teaches schoolchildren that France is the country of the golden mean, through which the 45th parallel runs, thus guaranteeing a temperate climate, this does not mean that it enjoys an even climate from one horizon to the other. Besides, how could that be so, since this small country is still the largest of Western Europe, with the exception of the Community of Independent States?

To this decidedly simplistic image of the hexagon, that of an open France is to be preferred, the image of a country that lies at the crossroads of every kind of geography on the continent. In loose lines, it actually summarizes all of Europe. There are the infinite plains of the north that come to die in Flanders. There is the old Hercynian plateau which frames the country from the rounded reliefs of Bretagne (Brittany) to the Ardennes, passing by the round-topped Vosges Mountains and the Plateaus of the Massif Central. More recent upheavals caused the Jura, the Alps, Corsica, and the Pyrenees to rise up into vivid ridges. One must not forget that on the geological scale it was only yesterday that the volcanic action of the Auvergne gave France the youngest of the mountains in Europe.

At this stage of the approach another element announces its presence, that of water. The erosion which shaped these reliefs, differently based on their age, lies also at the origin of the plains and basins which stud the territory of France. These low-lying regions, fertile and well-watered by the rivers and their tributaries, are the reason for the country's agricultural wealth, as for example the Parisian Basin which for a long time was the "wheat loft" of the kingdom. Plains are present in every region, even though they are sometimes tiny and lie at the bottom of a valley. Finally, between plain and mountain, criss-crossed by a thousand lively and quiet rivers, a world of hills lends itself to every human enterprise when not left in a natural state: olive grove or vineyard, meadow or forest, scrubland or ploughed fields, they form a fascinating kaleidoscope, sometimes playing on contrasts, sometimes on harmony.

When speaking of the geography of France, mention must be made of the coast in all its various aspects: winds, seasons, islands, lakes, canyons and cliffs, glaciers and abysses. But it is time to make the connection between these landscapes and the people that make them come alive. The French could not be confused with any other people, so specific is their personality. These people, though proud to be French, will with the same conviction confirm they are Breton, for example, and Bigouden (from the area of Pont-l'Abbé) before anything else, when they meet a Breton from another region. The French have wed the geography of their land through their traditional activities, shepherds here, fishermen there, miners, oyster farmers, salt merchants, caretakers, wine growers or foresters elsewhere. In the meantime, these people are also the product of twenty centuries of history, which they perpetuate through accents, physiognomies, specific habits and customs. We know that on the humus left behind by the people of Prehistory and by the great Celtic ancestors, the Germans, Romans, Normans, and other invaders settled, thereby constituting the common foundation of the French people and the basis for the present homogeneity of language, religion, and culture.

The French nation began to be shaped at the same time that the Roman colonization, so good at gaining Gallic experiences, took place. One of the great dates in French history, thereafter, was the year 843 in which the Treaty of Verdun was signed: this text, which determined the European borders for a long time to come, divided Charlemagne's empire into three kingdoms of equal importance. Among these, the ephemeral Francia occidentalis stretched from the North Sea to the Rhône delta. Once split up, this kingdom became reconstituted little by little during the twelfth and thirteenth centuries by the Capetian Kings who started with their possessions in Ile-de-France and to these added Champagne, Languedoc, and Normandy. The continuation of the formation of France, of such complexity that it delights historians, included marriages, wars, treaties, annexations, and bargaining sessions, the latter among the Capetians and the Valois, the Valois and the Bourbons.

In passing it should be noted that Roussillon was united with the kingdom in 1642, Franche-Comté in 1678, Lorraine in 1766, more than a century after Alsace, while Nivernais and Comtat Venaissin did not become French until 1789, just after Corsica did. In 1815, after the jolts of the Revolution and the Empire, France was thus defined by its present borders, except for the Savoie and Nice, which were annexed in 1860.

For those who know how to go beyond modern appearances, France remains in many ways a place composed of rather individualized provinces where they sometimes speak a "foreign" language, as in Corsica or in the Basque country, in Brittany or in Alsace. The old division between the north where the langue d'oïl was spoken and the south of the langue d'oc still remains in place as well through the various dialects, mentalities, and temperaments. Certain fratricidal confrontations of the past have even left vivid memories behind among the Huguenot communities of the Cévennes, in Vendée, or among the descendants of the Paolist shepherds of Corsica, for example.

Each French region has thus been cultivating its peculiarities since long ago, and at the present time, as Europe unites, this tendency is still active, as shown specifically by the Catalans. Discovering France, then, is to savour each of the provinces. It is learning to differentiate the Romanesque art of Normandy from that of the Auvergne or the Midi region around Toulouse, reading the country landscapes there where the regrouping of lands has not held sway, examining the traditional forms of architecture which are so well adapted to their environment, understanding why villages are perched atop a hill here and farms stand in isolation over there, finding the ancient roads of transhumance, smuggling, and commerce back again, and making the approach in such a way as to get to know the smallest French entity, that is to say the very soil itself.

At this point in the account, in order to appreciate the extraordinary diversity of France, its gastronomy should be taken into consideration. More than anywhere else, good food and wine are actually in harmony with the landscapes, and, seen in the light of this completely French art form, the country's geography takes on another dimension. One could travel here even if one's interest lies only in the cheeses – one for each day of the year, they say –, delicatessen, pastries or the wines. The latter category does not even exclude the northern and western provinces if one takes into consideration the gin, beers, ciders, and other forms of calvados produced there. . .

Approaching French reality through its cities is no less instructive. Historians make a distinction between the cities that have built their fortune on wine, like Reims, Bordeaux, Beaune, Dijon, Chalon-sur-Saône, Avignon, Narbonne, Béziers, and Montpellier. Others, equally prosperous, rose up around the harvesting of wheat: this is the way Flanders gathered its wealth, relying heavily on its proud belfries, while Ile-de-France built the Gothic spires of its cathedrals straight into the sky. Still other cities banked on commerce, such as Nantes, Lyon, Nancy or Marseille, and often relied on the administrative services of their lords who were counts, dukes or barons.

In modern times, industry, research, and the university have taken over, and certain cities have distinguished themselves in particular, for example Saint-Nazaire which had its hour of glory with the trans-Atlantic liners that came from its shipyards, Toulouse with its airplanes and rockets, Clermont-Ferrand with its tires, or Sochaux with its cars.

Among all these cities that history created Paris still occupies an incomparable place, to the point that one cannot blame some rushed visitors who think they can get an idea of France by visiting only the capital. Ever since the Capetian kings chose it as the seat of their power in the twelfth century, Paris has actually never stopped disseminating its political and intellectual influence across the country. This is translated through a profusion of exceptional monuments, spread across astonishingly diverse "landscapes" which make of Paris more than a single city. And furthermore, this goes hand in hand with innumerable historical, literary or artistic evocations, which are the very expression of the French spirit.

Literally, this is the spirit of rigorous Classicism to be seen on the façades of private townhouses or of the Louvre, or else that illustrated by Descartes, a philosopher who was not, it must be said, much of a Parisian. But in the collective imagination, primarily abroad, the French spirit is also that which presides over fashion shows, over the musical, pictorial or theatrical avant-gardes, and generally over all that the creative imagination offers in what is festive and sparkling with brilliance. Such is the immortal champagne-that-is-Paris for which the visitor hopes and which never disappoints.

Above: Cliffs of Cape Blanc Nez.
Opposite: Ice-sailing on the beach of Hardelo.
Upper right page: Ice-sailing on the beach of Sainte-Cécile.
Lower right page: Cliffs of Cape Gris Nez.

THE NORTHERN SHORES

Traveling the shores of Flanders and Artois is discovering these northern provinces under a much more varied light than one had imagined. From the long sandy strands of coastal Flanders, where nothing marks the frontier with Belgium, the visitor actually passes over to the chalk cliffs of Boulonnais and to the major natural monuments Blanc-Nez and Gris-Nez, then to the wild and mysterious stretches of Marquenterre and the Bay of the Somme. The cities of this coastline show a similar contrast: heroic and industrious Dunkerque (Dunkirk), Calais, the bridgehead to England, Boulogne, the capital of fishing, and Le Touquet which thinks of itself as the Beach of Paris but which is marked by an atmosphere that hails from across the Channel.

The role of the Opale coast as a seaside resort is well established, and from Bray-Dunes on the Belgian border to Fort-Mahon-Plage near the Somme, more than twenty resorts, for family, sports or the upper classes, come alive every summer. Yet, as the lines of cabanas or bright colored tents that line every beach suggest, the principal pleasures are not necessarily those of the water. Since the warm water and sunshine, offered by many places elsewhere, are lacking here, people like to play with the wind of which the coast of Opale is the kingdom. The waves, the strand, and the cliffs of the north thus see the blooming of windsurfing, storm sailing, kite-flying, delta-winged plane flying, and above all ice-sailing, which is the great local specialty.

FLANDRE, ARTOIS

One of the most striking features of the northern part of France is the density of its population, translated by landscapes shaped by mankind to their last detail. That is why the discovery of these French low lands is first of all the discovery of their cities, which are astonishingly rich in heritage considering how many wars have torn these horizons apart. Each northern city thus draws attention to itself through its vast square, seems a little overdone, in the images of the fairs, the patronal feasts or the carnivals. French Classicism, too, was reinterpreted in the fashion of Flanders, as were Art Nouveau and Art Deco later on.

Lille, the capital of the North, shows every facet of this urbanity with its Grand-Place, over which the former stockmarket reigns, typical of the Flemish Baroque with its neo-Flemish belfry and the buildings of the Place Louise-de-Bettignies, whose

Upper: The former Stockmarket on the Place Charles de Gaulle in Lille.
Above: The Grand Place in Arras.
Opposite: Façade of a building on the Place Louis de Bettignies in Lille.
Right page: The belfry in Lille.

stressing the opulence of yesteryear's middle classes with the help of its great many scrolled or stepped gables, aligned in tight rows. From the particularities of its Renaissance architecture, the visitor concludes that the past of this region lay at the crossroads of Flemish and Burgundian paths. One especially feels the North reveal its true nature through the decorative frenzies of the Flemish Baroque which sometimes

stories are protected from humidity by sandstone. As for Arras, it too is not to be outdone where the Flemish Baroque is concerned; its Grand-Place possesses a complete selection of this style.

PICARDIE

In bringing the Gothic style to its maturity, Picardie contributed an essential element to European culture. Nevertheless, in order for the cathedrals of Amiens and Beauvais to attain that degree of perfection which is theirs, the builders of the Middle Ages had to first establish the principles of Gothic art. The genre's model was Notre-Dame de Laon, a sanctuary so immediately successful that it was given "the Wonder of the West" as epithet.

The Gothic conventions are found in their entirety in the scope, the height, the balance, and the openness to light in this Laon cathedral. Here is an architectural majesty accompanied by a complete renewal of the decorative forms, although the famous monumental oxen that keep watch underneath the top of the turrets still evoke the colourfulness of Romanesque statuary. These sculptures were placed there in memory of an episode that occurred during the construction, one that would have ended badly had it not been for the quasi miraculous intervention of one of these animals. From the old Carolingian city of Laon to Soissons, forever associated with the episode of the famous vase, Picardie occupied an enviable place in the early beginnings of French history. For a long time, the province remained close to the seat of power as Compiègne symbolizes, which marked the summit of the Second Empire after that of the Ancien Régime. During this transition, the Château of Louis XV, restored and converted by Napoleon I, was a showcase for the best of the Empire style, where the bedroom of the emperor may indeed be seen.

Upper left page: Former Episcopal Palace in Beauvais.
Lower left page: Bedroom of Napoleon I in the Château de Compiègne.
Above: View of the city of Laon.
Opposite: Detail of the tower of the Laon cathedral.

HAUTE-NORMANDIE

"La reprise monotone du roulement de la douce houle use et polit indéfiniment..." ("The monotonous resumption of the gentle swell's rumbling unendingly wears away and polishes . . .") Paul Valéry wrote about the Alabaster Coast.

In that way the writer took his place among the group of artists who sang the praises or laid down on canvas the most beautiful of the natural landscapes of Haute-Normandie,

after Corot, Courbet, Monet or Maupassant. Born in Fécamp, the latter was one of the pioneers of Étretat, an unknown fishing village whose extraordinary setting was discovered belatedly – "you'd think an elephant was plunging its trunk into the sea", he said about the Porte d'Aval. As his house, "La Guillette" was being built, he contributed to the early success of Étretat as a resort and became one of the first "old timers", that is to say one of its

Above: Chalk cliffs on the edges of Dieppe.
Opposite: Château Gaillard.
Upper right: Cliffs at Étretat.
Lower right: Cliff of Amont at Étretat.

Overleaf: Abbaye aux Hommes in Caen.

longstanding summer residents. From the surroundings of Dieppe, where they overhang the Channel, to the interior borders of the province, the chalk cliffs punctuate most of the horizons of Normandy. Whether along the shore or in the interior, when they run along a coveted passage, they have invariably been placed to the advantage of the establishment of a stronghold; in this regard, one of the best examples is Château-Gaillard, which dominates the Seine River on the borders of Vexin. This fortress was built in one year by Richard Lionheart who wanted to bar Philip Augustus from using the road to Rouen. Château-Gaillard extended the Andelys cliffs with walls that were considered impregnable, at least until Philip Augustus attacked this much coveted key to Normandy and swept it away.

BASSE-NORMANDIE

Caen, today's capital of Basse-Normandie, owes everything to the greatest figure of the province, Guillaume le Bâtard (William the Bastard). The chain of events deserves to be told, for it explains how the city found itself endowed with two of the most beautiful sanctuaries of the province.

Guillaume, the young and spirited Duke of Normandy, born in Falaise but preferring to live in Caen, had married Mathilde de Flandres without having asked for the papal dispensation which their distant blood relationship required. This resulted in a serious disagreement with the Church, which the couple managed to resolve in return for the founding of two abbeys. Thus, in 1063, Guillaume ordered the construction of the Abbaye aux Hommes (the Abbey of Men), while Mathilde presided over that of the Abbaye aux Dames (the Abbey of Ladies). The two establishments enjoyed an exemplary destiny, which can be measured by the majestic development of their monastic buildings, redone in the eighteenth century. Their abbeys, the Saint-Étienne and Trinité Churches, on the other hand, still stand as a precious testimony to the Romanesque art of Normandy brought to its highest point of perfection. The whole beauty of the buildings lies in the accuracy of its proportions, the expert distribution of its openings, and the perfectionism of the work of the master masons, to the exclusion of any decoration. In expressing the ducal faith, these churches also symbolize the power of a sovereign who was to become, a few years later, Guillaume le Conquérant (William the Conqueror), while his spouse would become Queen Mathilde.

17

NORTHERN BRETAGNE, FINISTERE

When one thinks of Bretagne, images of ruggedness come to mind. Chapels of granite battered by the winds, lighthouses beleaguered by the elements, and with that the sailors who are as pious as they are courageous. Promontories that stick out like wedges between the Atlantic and the Channel, islands cut off from the rest of the world, and always the sailors, equal to none, as

another amidst which humankind has no place. Its place, when found, is created by becoming one with the omnipresent granite, whether that be a minute shelter of fishermen between two rocks or the most proud of pirate cities, in the image of Saint-Malo.

Thus situated, Saint-Malo could only devote itself to the sea, and its citizens participated in every expedition to the distant West, New Foundland, Canada, and Spanish America,

Above: The pink granite coast at Ploumanac'h.
Opposite: Aerial view of Saint Malo.
Below: Lighthouse at Ploumanac'h.
Right page: The Point du Raz.

fine as fishermen as they used to be formidable as pirates.

This Celtic land, whose view over the open sea never ends, this province of magic spells and eternal myths, possesses a supplementary soul in some places which makes it different from everything known elsewhere in France. Such is the case of the pink granite coast, at Ploumanac'h, where the shore seems inhabited by mastodons from another world, while at the Pointe du Raz one thinks one is present at a moment in Genesis when elements confront one

nor did they fail to rush upon the English when the opportunity presented itself. Is it not striking to what extent this city resembles a ship ready to cast off its cables from the continent?

SOUTHERN BRETAGNE

In southern Bretagne, the power of nature is welcoming, especially in the vicinity of Concarneau, Quiberon, and the Gulf of Morbihan. The water often takes on the colour of tropical seas and the sand of the beaches is warm. There, too, one finds the sailors, and still just as fearsome since they compete in regattas... The primary business, however, is still fishing, with Concarneau and Lorient the main ports; shrines are found in the many picturesque harbours which dot the shoreline from Audierne to Pornic, while passing through Étel and its curious interior sea.

As on the northern coast of Bretagne, oysterfarming also figures among the marine professions. The principal region of production is the Gulf of Morbihan, an astonishing

universe in which land and sea sketch out a puzzle which every tide designs anew. Around this paradise of birds and pleasure boats are some of the great centres of interest of southern Bretagne, such as the historic cities of Vannes and Auray, such as the alignments of the menhirs of Carnac or the long peninsula of Quiberon.

The islands of this sunny Bretagne are a reflection of its coast; the bright character of Belle-Ile, for example, responds to the Finistère austerity of the islands of Sein. The largest of the Breton islands certainly has a savage coast where it faces the sea, but that is undoubtedly to exploit the Mediterranean vegetation which surrounds Le Palais and Sauzon, the picturesque and colourful ports on the other side.

Upper left page: Larmor-Baden in the Gulf of Morbihan.
Lower left: The river Etel.
Above and opposite: The harbour of Sauzon at Belle-Ile.

THE ESTUARY OF THE LOIRE

Somewhat in the style of Nantes, which is both eminently Breton and very jealous of its own identity, the regions that run along the Loire Estuary display such originality that they seem to live on the margins of the province. For Brière and the region of Guérande even more so than for the region of Retz, this isolation is first of all of a geographic nature. The Grande Brière, which forms the second largest group of marshes in France after the Camargue, corresponds to one of the phases of the filling in of a seaside gulf that probably used to resemble the Gulf of Morbihan. Since the Middle Ages, the natural process has been exploited by man, or rather by a specific race of men, the Briérons. The inalienable property of its inhabitants since the fifteenth century,

Top: The Grande Brière.
Above and lower right page:
Salt marshes of Guérande.
Upper right: Pond of Saudun in the
Grande Brière.

Grande Brière provides them with peat for heating, hay from the marshes for the cattle, reeds for the rooftops of their cottages, sludge to enrich the soil of the gardens, without counting hunting and fishing which certainly improve the everyday. Flowing from all this is a very specific lifestyle, as original as that of the workers in the salt marshes of Guérande, the neighbours of the Briérons.

In fact, the salty marshes, that made the fortune of Guérande, the "Breton Carcassonne", also continue to maintain a picturesque tradition. The setting of Guérande is made of a mosaic of shimmering ponds in which the ocean's water is turned into salt, this precious commodity which the workers of the salt marshes come to "pick" with their "rakes" before stacking it into small brilliant heaps, the "mulons".

MAINE, ANJOU

Enlarged by the Vienne, the Loire River in Anjou takes on a new scope and its Val becomes a gentle valley of legendary sweetness. The river and its tributaries flow throughout the history of France, from Joan of Arc at Chinon, to Saint Louis at Angers, while literary references that are attached to its current reflect what is best of a certain French culture, from Rabelais to la Devinière, from Du Bellay to the "petit Liré".

The great Châteaux stretch along this part of the Loire naturally, such as for example at Angers and Saumur – opposite, the sixteenth century town hall of Saumur. Yet, more than in Touraine and Orléanais, there are innumerable spots that embellish the borders of the region, from the boundaries of Bretagne to those of Poitou. Thus, in Maine, between Sarthe and Mayenne, there stands one of the most enticing châteaux of the Loire, for want of being one of the most prestigious. Indeed, Le Plessis-Bourré appears, in the middle of its wide moats, as a pleasure fortress dressed in micaceous chalk and slate, austere exteriors that hide the esoteric and opulent rooms of a royal counselor fascinated by the occult sciences.

The divine spirit also whispers across these horizons, and two symbols are an illustration thereof, the Abbaye de Fontevraud, an extraordinary monastic grouping, which was always placed under royal protection, and that of Solesmes, which occupies an incomparable place in the heart of modern Christianity.

Left page: Château de Saumur.
Upper: Château du Plessis-Bourré.
Above left: Abbey of Fontevrault: the Sainte-Marie Cloister.
Above right: Abbey of Solesmes: detail of the entombment of Christ.

TOURAINE, ORLÉANAIS

Touraine is above all else the "Valley of the châteaux", where under a luminous sky the Loire and its retinue of tributaries, originating in the Massif Central, wash along some of the major monuments of the French cultural heritage. If one were made to retain only one image of this eternal France, it might be that of Chenonceaux, this "ladies' château", the glory of which was made by Diane de Poitiers and Catherine de Médicis. The extraordinary grand gallery, which straddles the water of the Cher in the extension of the initial château, was actually an undertaking of Henri II's favorite, before she was thrown out by the king's widow, who was determined to continue the work of her rival. In this Val de Loire, the "garden of France", the Château de Blois occupies a pri-

vileged place, for it is, all by itself, a summary of the history of the fleur-de-lys ornamented architecture. The hall of the States General illustrates the Middle Ages of the counts, the Louis XII wing shows the last sparks of the Gothic, the part erected by François I bears witness to an as yet faltering Renaissance, and finally the main residential area of Gaston d'Orléans imprints Blois with the markings of a Classicism that is no longer a copy of the model from across the Alps. In the same range of slightly cold elegance and of lofty harmony, typical of the classical style, the Château de Cheverny rises on the edge of Sologne's well-stocked game forests: this dwelling was thus designed completely for the perpetuation of the hunting traditions in their most brilliant form.

Left page: Château de Blois.

Above: Château de Chenonceau.

Opposite: Château de Cheverny.

VENDÉE, POITOU

The creation of Futuroscope Park, in 1987, in the area surrounding Poitiers, put the spotlight on a region that until then had been unknown. For Poitou is part of those French provinces of whose discreet charms the true beauty is not grasped until after a long acquaintanceship. Suddenly surging up from the land, following the example of the giant crystal which is its symbol, Futuroscope has made Poitou's image more dynamic by making its capital the pioneer of future technologies. Next to an amusement park and a training complex, which is closely connected to an industrial site, the most spectacular aspect of Futuroscope is concerned with the cinema of the next century. And already its seats reach out to spectators for sessions that make them tremble...

Closely related to Poitou in many ways, Vendée is nevertheless known primarily because of its coast,

Above and centre right page: Futuroscope in Poitiers.
Opposite: The harbour of Sables-d'Olonne.
Upper right page: The harbour of the island of Yeu.

28

because of its seaside resorts. The coastal cliff road of Vendée, long sandy shores, and islands in the sea make up this world, washed by the ocean and animated by a few fishing harbours throughout the year. The largest flotilla is that of Sables-d'Olonne, a providential open harbour in the middle of a low-lying coast that is hostile to navigation. Now attached to the shore by a highway bridge, the island of Noirmoutier is thus more favourable to the growing of fresh produce than to fishing. Very different from this is the island of Yeu which, far into the sea, evokes the image of a Breton piece of granite lost in the south, and lies arranged around the beautiful seaside village of Port-Joinville.

AUNIS

La Rochelle, the capital of Aunis, is an historic city that lays claim to the title of most beautiful harbour of France. This is no idle boast, if one is to judge by the number of painters who have put the famous towers of the Vieux Port on canvas. Lovers of fine food, particularly of seafood, also lavish their highest praise on La Rochelle, and even if one limits one-self to its most inland aspects, the city must be placed in the ranks of

Colbert, was the birthplace of Julien Viaud in 1850. Although its maritime destiny had been fairly modest, Rochefort did commercial business across the seven seas, to the point that, enthralled by the vision of the ships that came from distant horizons, Julien Viaud became a navy officer with the intendion of seeing the world. After his return, this child of Rochefort, delved into his experiences and published innumerable novels under the pseudonym Pierre

Upper: Rochefort: the Renaissance room in the house of Pierre Loti.

Above: La Rochelle: the Hôtel de Ville.

Right page: Rochefort: the Turkish salon in the house of Pierre Loti.

the great tourist routes. Its prestigious past, especially the period during which it was the main commercial port for Canada, brought La Rochelle the opportunity to be filled with buildings worthy of a capital. Thus, enthroned among masses of superb private townhouses, a city hall emerges, the Henri IV façade of which is a high point of refinement. Rochefort, a harbour of Aunis made the equal of Brest and Toulon by

Loti. This name, taken from a small Tahitian flower, translated an unquenchable thirst for exoticism which the writer attempted to satisfy by transforming the family home into a kind of fantastic museum, which allowed him to travel both in time and space.

ANGOUMOIS AND SAINTONGE

From the "green Venice" of Poitou to the marshes of Gironde, the department of Charente-Maritime sees its shores spangled with amphibious stretches on which the ocean and the continent celebrate a strange wedding. Produced by the fluctuations of the sea level and the alluvial deposits of the rivers, these areas were all colonized to various ends by man. Here and there in the passage of Oléron, across which runs an impressive cement viaduct, the landscape is thus completely covered with marshes and oyster beds. The cradle of French oysterfarming and the first centre of production of the continent, the Marennes-Oléron basin produces up to 50.000 tons of oysters every year.

It is known that Saintonge was one of the chosen regions of Romanesque art and, seen from that point of view, the Eglise de Sainte-Radegonde de Talmont is the jewel of the province, eclipsing even the great sanctuaries. Beautifully situated on the edge of the highway along the Gironde, and linked to a delightful village whose houses vie with each other in hollyhocks, this church used to mark a point of embarkation on the road of pilgrimage to San Juan de Compostela. The church itself is "endangered by the sea", and just recently it had to have its rocky foundations strengthened, beaten by the waters of the estuary. Pilgrims, entering through the north portal, used to read the Biblical episodes that would underlie their quest, right on the stones, before they would find the characters on the nave's capitals.

Upper left page and opposite:
The Sainte Radegonde de Talmont
Church.
Lower left page and above:
Oysterfarms in Marennes-Oléron.

LIMOUSIN, BERRY, BOURBONNAIS

As they discover the name of the plateau of Millevaches (i.e. a thousand cows) on a map, many foreigners must have smiled, thinking of the Limousin farmers who are all too inclined to counting their livestock. Reality is very different, since what is enumerated on this high granite land are the "batz", otherwise known as the springs, according to the Celtic terminology. These one thousand batz, sometimes growing languid in limpid ponds, sometimes cascading towards the Vézère, the Corrèze, the Creuse, the Thaurion, the Vienne, the Maulde, and the Diège, illustrate the role of the water tower of France which the geographers have attributed to the Massif Central, as everyone has learned at school.

For the geographers also, it is in Limousin and Bourbonnais that the regions of Northern France and

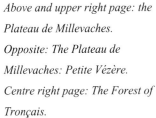

Above and upper right page: the Plateau de Millevaches.
Opposite: The Plateau de Millevaches: Petite Vézère.
Centre right page: The Forest of Tronçais.

Southern France encounter each other, a border that in olden days became concrete through the speech of the langue d'oïl and the langue d'oc, and even today is visible in the roofs of slate or flat tiles and those of round tiles. Between Berry and Bourbonnais, one of the contact points between these cultures is the Forest of Tronçais, famous for its three hundred-year old oak trees, planted on Colbert's initiative. Its wood is used in cabinetmaking, but also serves for the making of the barrels used for the aging of the Bordeaux wines and cognac. The Forest of Tronçais, studded with ponds and picturesques sites, is similarly well-known for its fauna – stags, does, deer, boar – and for its wealth of flavourful mushrooms, especially boletus and chanterelles.

AUVERGNE

The old Gallic land which Vercinge-torix made into the cradle of national identity, the Auvergne preserves the memory of a distant Celtic occupation in its name. "Arvern" is the region of summits, modest culminating points when compared to those of the Alps or the Pyrenees, but most impressive for those who watched them emerge, smoking and spitting fire from the entrails of the planet. Indeed, among the volcanoes of the which reach beyond 1800 meters, on the other hand, are the ruined witnesses of much more ancient volcanoes. These complex structures, whose immensity outshines that of Etna, were hollowed out of deep valleys created by the glaciers of the Quaternary era. They make up a pastoral universe filled with forests and of innumerable variants, which man has long known how to tame. The hot water springs were already appreciated by the Romans. The

Auvergne are to be found the youngest mountains of the Hexagon, which were contemporaries with the ancestors from Prehistory. The craters aligned with the chain of the Puys, the cliffs of columnar basalt, as well as several very deep and perfectly round lakes, emphasize the origin of the land of volcanoes.

The true summits of Auvergne, the Puy de Sancy, the sheer plummet of Cantal, and the parade of ridges steep lava peaks have almost all been embellished with feudal squares or Romanesque sanctuaries where Virgins as black as the basalt itself are adored. And today, once winter has arrived, the pastureland up high becomes the playground of skiers.

Upper: Puy Mary: the small lake.
Above: the Plomb du Cantal.
Opposite: Tilestone rock.
Right page: The Monts Dorés and
the Château de Murol.

PÉRIGORD

Traditionally, the Périgord is described according to its colours. The white Périgord is the one that forms the centre of the province and has the brilliance of the cliffs in which mankind sought shelter in the time of the war of fire. This whiteness, or rather this blondeness of the limestone can be found again in most of the monuments, both in the Roman vestiges, of which the Tower of Vésone is the example, and in the string of castles that escort the current of the Dordogne River.

The black Périgord received its name because of the dark leaves of the oaks which cover the south-east of the region. But one might also wish to see an allusion to the "black diamond" of Périgord gastronomy, the truffle, whose winter harvest calls upon subtleties known only by the initiated. The province's markets contribute more than their part with ducks and geese, who turn up at fine meals in the form of magret, conserve or foies gras.

A special mention should be made of the regional wines, of which Monbazillac is the flagbearer. Recently, the colour of the grapes in the vineyards around Bergerac has served, furthermore, to baptize the western regions of the province, where they foreshadow Bordelais, with the name of the purple Périgord. To complete the picture, the most Limousin part of the Dordogne department was named the green Périgord at the same time, made very green indeed by a number of waterways that come from the Massif Central.

Upper left page: Sign in Sarlat.
Lower left page: Truffle market.
Above: The Vésone tower in Périgueux.
Opposite: Looking for truffles.
Overleaf: Cave paintings in Lascaux.

QUERCY

A cousin of the Périgord, Quercy is no less well endowed with prehistoric riches or sites weighed down by history, while the banks of the Lot also can take on a comparison with those of the Dordogne, just as the wine of Cahors can compete with that of Bergerac. Though it is visited relatively little, outside of a few prestigious spots, Quercy nevertheless conceals seductive treasures, of which the foodlover alone can give an idea: here also there are truffles and foies gras, here too are boletus, morels, nuts, lambs from the limestone plateaus, trout, and goat cheese, to mention but a few of the region's specialties.

Forming a pair with the natural wonders of the chasm of Padirac, the other grand tourist site of Quercy, Rocamadour makes an impression with its setting as much as with its spiritual dimension. For a thousand years, and still today, this site of the gorges of Alzou sees pilgrims of every background pass by, miserable wretches and crowned heads, who have come to gather on the tomb of Saint Amadour and before an ancient black Virgin, in the hope they will hear the bell that signals a miracle as it rings by itself. Similarly, it is by climbing on foot that visitors discover Saint-Cirq-Lapopie, one of France's most beautiful villages, that hangs suspended from an escarpment on the banks of the Lot. The little cobblestone streets show the village's half-timbered houses, restored by artists or craftsmen, while from the church's terrace or from the ruins of the castle that stands above the cliff, superb panoramic views over the river can be seen.

Left page and above left: The village of Saint Cirq Lapopie.
Upper: Rocamadour.
Above right: Cahors: dovecote.

43

Above: Wine harvest in the region of Pessac of Château Haut Brion.
Opposite: Château Margaux: The plant.
Upper right page: Château Margaux: The storehouse.
Lower right page: Château Margaux.
Overleaf: Saint Emilion.

BORDEAUX AND ITS VINEYARDS

In the eyes of the world, Bordeaux is less a city than a collection of great wines, some of which reach the sublime. It is true that the city was born in the Roman era at the same time as its vineyard. It is equally true that this port on the Atlantic would not have known the destiny that was to be its own, had it not been for the ships that came from very far away to load the precious casks of Bordeaux wines. By its very countenance, the city evokes the fortune made by wine dealers, as can be seen in the district of the Chartrons, where the rhythm of activity is still indicated by the seasons of viticulture, even if it is no longer as glaring as it once was. Then, the huge bell at the top of one of the medieval gates of the city would ring on the occasion of great events, especially to announce the "proclamation of the vintage". In any case, before the suburbs of Bordeaux end one sees the beginning of the vineyards, and not the least important one at that, since the renowned Château Haut-Brion, vineyard of one of the fine wines, is closest to the heart of the Aquitaine capital. Sauternes, Saint-Émilion, Pornerol or Fronsac are also part of the aristocracy of the Bordeaux wines, but where they are concerned it is again at the gates of the city, on the Médoc side, that the best of their production is found, particularly with the immensely famous Château Margaux. First among the great wines of the Médoc, this prince of wines has as his companions the Château Lafite-Rothschild, the Château Latour, and the Château Mouton-Rothschild.

AQUITAINE

In passing from the Bordeaux region into Aquitaine, one does not leave the universe of the great dated wines. To manufacture these, the producers learned how to wed secular traditions to the most advanced techniques in such a way that the gustatory qualities improved even further. Interior Aquitaine lies outside the beaten path of tourism, yet, as is often the case, it appears like a land of plenty. From Agenais to the Baïse, thus recalls the memory of the d'Albret family. Starting with this fiefdom, as modest today as it was yesterday, the Gascon princes little by little became the greatest feudal lords of the south-west, and under the influence of Marguerite d'Angoulême, the Court of Nérac was the main intellectual centre of Aquitaine. Jeanne d'Albret, Queen of Navarre and mother of Henri IV, later made this city into one of the bastions of Protestantism. Next to a

Above: Stainless steel vat.
Opposite: Outbuildings of the
Château Lafitte-Rothschild.
Below: Bottles of Château
Beychevelle.
Right page: Aerial view of Nérac.

Armagnac, the masterword is that of good living, whether that be at a table where a meat pie or a ragout of game is to be shared, around a grassy field in suspense over a soccer match, or for the occasion of a simple village festival.

Moreover, when names such as Agen, Villeneuve-sur-Lot or Labastide-d'Armagnac are mentioned, the measure of what this region owes to its past in terms of national heritage and culture becomes obvious. Nérac, to name another of these historic cities, on the banks of castle touched by history, Nérac thus preserves a warren that is the former royal park where, close to a fountain, the future king of France met Fleurette, his first love.

COTE LANDAISE

Until the last century, the Landes was a vast, boggy, and unhealthy region, separated from the sea by a line of dunes. Hardly anything is left from this period except the stilts, once used to allow the shepherds to keep their feet dry, which are part of the traditional costume of the Landes. Since the region has been transformed by the large-scale plantations of pine-trees, even a new tradition has had time to be born and to disappear, namely the harvest of resin in small earthenware pots, attached to every trunk just below where a notch was cut into the tree. The main element of the natural regional park of the Landes de Gascogne, which may be reached thanks to a small steam train, equally a survivor of this recent past, is the Ecomuseum of Marquèze. Its mission is to present the traditional life of the Landes which people might otherwise forget because of the tourist trade in the seaside resorts. The flower of this new attraction is, of course, Arcachon, a small and quiet fishing port that has become the elegant summer residence of the inhabitants of Bordeaux. It reigns over a plethora of more family oriented seaside towns, that lie along the hundreds of kilometres of this sandy coastline, which is far from monotonous, however.

Two examples prove the opposite. The major natural curiosity of the region is the Dune of Pilat, which dominates over the passages of the basin of Arcachon from its height of 114 meters, a record in Europe, while, hidden further south between the lake of Léon and Moliets-Plage, the Huchet waterway has every appearance of an equatorial river.

Left page: A forest in Landes.
Above and overleaf: The Dune de Pilat.
Opposite: Waterside at Huchet.

51

PAYS BASQUE

The Basque country is a strange area, that goes without saying. It is the region of a people whose origins are unknown, but which prides itself on being the oldest in Europe. All they need to do is create "modern" borders. Their language, euskera, is related to no other tongue. Having come through the centuries preserving the isolation which the Pyrenees chain allowed them to have, the Basques have quite naturally developed traditions and lifestyles whose originality is of the finest sort.

It is known that pelota is the favorite sport of the Basques, who revere the great players like heroes and who couldn't live without having a fronton within sight. Almost as important in the culture of this region are the folkloric dances, most often reserved for men, which similarly provide them with an opportunity to prove their agility, power, and concentration. Beyond these invariables, the different Basque provinces each have their own personality, as a saying stresses: "The people from Soule are dancers, those from Navarre write verse, and those from Labourd are the pelota players."

From Adour to Bidassoa, the Basque coast distinguishes itself by a tourist trade that very early on complemented the traditional fishing activities. After having been the resort of the aristocracy, Biarritz has become a surfers' paradise; Saint-Jean-de-Luz, perfect for swimming, remains an animated fishing harbour; and Hendaye, the frontier town, is watching its renown grow as a climatic and seaside resort.

Upper: Biarritz: the great beach and the Hôtel du Palais.
Above left: Saint-Jean-Pied-de-Port: the Rue de la Citadelle.

Above right: Fishing net in Saint-Jean-de-Luz.
Right page: Harbour of Saint-Jean-de-Luz.

BÉARN

Béarn shows very different facets from its 2885 meter peak of the Midi d'Ossau to the region of mountain torrents and in Adour. In the heart of the Pyrenees, the Béarn valleys, easily accessible but quite isolated one from the other, have been favorable to the development of vigourous, pastoral communities. Beyond the characteristics they have in common, such as powerful houses with walls of stone and pointed roofs of slate, traditional costumes, and the béarnaise language, they preserve their uniqueness. In contrast, in the region of the water torrents, the houses are low and covered with spouted tiles that connect with the sunny skies. This land of hills is also the land of corn and, better yet, of the Jurançon wine. This white wine had as its first claim to glory the fact that it served to baptize the future King Henri IV, the most famous figure of Béarn. Obviously this took place in Pau, in the castle shaped by history, around which grew the capital of the province.

On foundations that go back at least to the twelfth century, this palace was ceaselessly embellished and preserves the insignia of innumerable personalities of distinction, from Gaston Phébus to Napoleon III. Housed there now is the National Museum, linked to remembrances of Henri IV throughout several rooms that have remained unchanged since the sixteenth century, but especially by the addition of objects that have become famous, even adored, such as relics like his cradle of tortoise shell. Another one of the treasures of the museum is the monumental bed of Jeanne d'Albret.

Left page: Château de Pau: The bedroom of Jeanne d'Albret.
Above: Château de Pau.
Opposite: Houses typical of the village of Pau.

Above: The peak of Néouvielle and the Lac d' Aumar.

Right page, upper left: Stream in the valley of Marcadau.

Right, upper right: The peak of the Midi de Bigorre.

Lower right: Aerial view of the citadel of Montségur.

Overleaf: Cirque de Gavarnie.

THE PYRENEES

From the rocks of Biarritz to those of Collioure, the Pyrenees stretch across 400 kilometers in length in a barrier that is difficult to cross, but whose aspects offer an astonishing variety. In passing from the Atlantic to the Mediterranean, this cordillera of clear waters runs from the expansion of vegetation and the rich pastures of the Basque country to the vineyards and the perfumed scrub land of Catalonia. On the strongest of its mountains, the chain aligns summits that need not pale in comparison with the giants of the Alps and has sites that are strictly its own, such as the famous amphi-theatres, of which Gavarnie is the most well-known. And the remar-kable fauna has not even been men-tioned yet, over which it is hoped the bear will continue to reign: that is one of the objectives of the national park of the Pyrenees, a sanctuary of wild life and natural beauty.

Before reaching these inhospitable heights, the Pyrenees foothills are fol-lowed by gentle regions upon which mankind had put its mark very early on. The history written there begins with the great ancestors who lived in the caves of Lombrives, Niaux, and Mas-d'Azil. One of the most striking episodes here was the development of the Catharist faith, a reflection of the refined culture and the ideals that were prevalent in the Midi Pyrenees during the Middle Ages. Persecuted by the crusade led against them by the barons of the north, the "heretics" fled deeper and deeper into the moun-tains before they ended up by suc-cumbing to the numbers of their per-secutors. The citadel of Montségur will remain forever the symbol of their struggle.

THE MIDI PYRENEES

At first glance, the Midi Pyrenees do not seem to be as rich in great, sacred Medieval monuments as the other French provinces. Nevertheless, with the Saint-Sernin Basilica of Toulouse, the region possesses the largest and the most complete of the Romanesque churches in France. Devoted to Saint Saturnin, the first bishop of the city, this sanctuary translates the renewal of faith in the eleventh and twelfth centuries, and is of such a dimension that it could handle the masses of pilgrims who came to venerate the relics, as well as the impressive religious community that practised in Toulouse. Admirable because of its architectural lay-out that makes it into a crescendo of stone and brick cast up toward the sky, the Saint-Sernin Basilica is equally admirable because of its decoration, of which the sculptures around the Miégeville door are the jewels.

Moissac also belongs to this first Romanesque period. It was one of the great stops on the road to San Juan de Compostela. With the one at Saint-Sernin, the workshop of Moissac formed the basis for the blooming of Romanesque sculpture in Languedoc. More than the abbey church of Moissac, remarkable though it be, it is the cloister that makes the city worthy of being entered into the history of art: it, too, is the most important and most beautiful building of its genre to have remained in place, precious as much for the harmony of its order as for the richness of its setting. In the meantime, Gothic art also flowered in Languedoc, witness the former Notre-Dame de Saint-Bernard-de-Comminges Cathedral which stands enthroned on the "Mont-Saint-Michel des terres".

Left page: The cloister of Moissac.
Upper: St. Bertrand de Comminges.
Above: Aerial view of Montauban.

*Above: Albi: Aerial view of the old
city and of the Sainte Cécile
cathedral.*

*Opposite: Albi: Episcopal Palace of
Berbie.*

*Lower right page: Old sections of
Albi.*

*Upper right page: The rose window
of the Notre-Dame cathedral in
Rodez.*

ROUERGUE AND ALBIGEOIS

Resembling the department of Aveyron rather closely, Rouergue is a Languedoc region that remained marginal for a long time, for the roads that led there were far from comfortable. Those routes served rather for a departure from the area, which today has as many inhabitants as emigrants. Yet, all of them are passionately attached to their native Rouergue, whose landscapes and cities are very seductive, it must be said. In history, two cities on the banks of the Aveyron argue over the preeminence they hold over the province, Villefranche-de-Rouergue and Rodez. They clashed through interposed cathedrals, and Villefranche lost the game, having overrated its power as shown by the colossal foundations of a bell-tower porch that was never finished. In Rodez, on the façade and the bell-tower of the Notre-Dame Cathedral, the flaming Gothic style was then able to bring triumph to the red sandstone characteristic of the region. Further south, in Albigeois, the red that dominates is the red of brick and, in the heart of the capital of this region, the cathedral did not serve local ambition, but rather that of a Church badly hurt by the Catharist heresy. The grandiose cathedral of Sainte-Cécile d'Albi, with its bell-tower shaped like a donjon, and the episcopal Palace of Berbie that flanks it thus were the symbols of the power that had come to the rescue of truth, a power that for a long time was synonymous with the Inquisition. Now devoted to Toulouse-Lautrec, the most illustrious of Albi's children, the Palace of Berbie is henceforth the seat of more joyous evocations.

ROUSSILLON

A true region of crossroads, meeting-ground of the roads from the Iberian Peninsula, the ocean, the Rhône Valley, and Italy, Roussillon is obviously a land of transit. This is equally true for the anonymous traveler, the members of high society or the artists who left the province a heritage as rich as it is varied, but it was not any less true for the conquerors and their armies, in the tracks left by Hannibal and his elephants, or those of the Barbarians who came from the four corners of the world and even from the sea.

The northern door of Roussillon and the Catalan regions, Salses-le-Château was called upon to play a great role in this context. Its surprising fortress of stone and brick began to be constructed in 1497 on the orders of Ferdinand II of Castile, and it quickly became one of the keystones of the kingdom of Spain. First the French assailants ran into trouble there or decided that it was better to go around it. Then from surprise attacks to interminable sieges, the place changed hands several times before the annexation of Roussillon to France, with the Treaty of the Pyrenees of 1659, made it useless. And if the Château de Salses is today one of the major testimonies to military architecture at the transition from the Middle Ages to the era in which artillery triumphed, it is because the exceptional ruggedness of its structure discouraged any attempt at dismantling it ...

Opposite: Fortress of Salses-le-Château.

BAS-LANGUEDOC

In making a distinction between the Midi Pyrenees and Languedoc-Roussillon, modern regional differences have introduced a boundary which is not that of history. Indeed, Bas-Languedoc, especially the department of Aude, has maintained special bonds with Toulouse, Albi or Foix since a very long time ago, rather well concealed by the notion of the Catharist area, still anchored deeply in the mentality. What better symbol of this than the city of Carcassonne, which stands as if frozen in its medieval armour to symbolize the Languedoc resistance in its confrontation with the Albigensian crusade? At the same time, it must be recognized that the most extensive fortified city of the continent was, in another period, above all the main base of operations of the royalty as it took control over the Midi. Having also come under the domination of France's crown after the crusade, Minervois, which stands on the borders of Hérault today, was another of the strongholds of Catharism.

The extraordinary village of Minerve is its capital, entrenched between two gorges and evoking the image of an oasis lost in the middle of the limestone plateau, it capitulated only after a merciless siege by Simon de Montfort. The first Catharist stake was set afire in that town. If a place were needed as a counterpoint to Minerve, it might well be the beautiful Cistercian abbey of Fonfroide, from which Pierre de Castelnau left to preach against the heretics, and in which the papal legate, Arnaud-Amaury, died, who was the author of the appalling slogan "Kill them all, God shall recognize his own!"

Left page: The village of Minerve.
Above: The Porte d'Aude in
Carcassonne.
Opposite: The Abbey of Fontfroide.

HAUT-LANGUEDOC

Calling to mind Montpellier and Nîmes, the main cities of Haut-Languedoc, is going back in Western architectural history by going from the ambitious contemporary achievements of Montpellier to the prestigious roots of Nîmes, which still stands decked out in all of its "French Roman" attributes.

In contrast to the other Langeudoc cities, Montpellier was created fairly recently – it has just celebrated its

the style of several local architects of talent, in particular of Daviler, whose arcades have a characteristic shape. Recently, the proud regional hotel Polygone and other equally brilliant complexes have come to confirm the role Montpellier plans to play, which is that of the "beating heart of Languedoc".

Nîmes, its old rival, has gone a step further by constructing a very modern Carré d'Art close to its extremely famous Maison Carrée.

first millenium – which did not prevent it from winning fame precociously. First of all a seaport, Montpellier became rich through trade in spices and other herbs, which inspired the creation of Europe's first medical school within its walls. Then the city became the administrative capital of the province in the seventeenth century, a period during which it constructed vast numbers of superb buildings. One recognizes

In doing so, the city of festivals and bullfights, but also of the soothing garden of La Fontaine, confirms its desire to become a centre of contemporary creation. Still, one may bet that Nîmes will retain its image as a Roman city, so heavily does the presence of the arenas, the Maison Carrée, and the Gate of Augustus weigh upon its urban landscape.

Left page: The Hôtel de Région in Montpellier.
Upper: The Hôtel Montcalm in Montpellier.
Above: Arenas in Nîmes.
Opposite: The Hôtel Rodez Benavent in Montpellier.

VELAY, CÉVENNES, CAUSSES

The volcanism of the Massif Central is not limited to the peaks incorporated in the Parc des Volcans of Auvergne, nor is it particularly well known that its manifestations appear all the way to the banks of the Rhône, in the Coirons, and even on the Mediterranean coast near Agde. Volcanism is also the origin of the astonishing sites of Velay, especially that of Puy. A unique atmosphere emanates from this old Marian city, a visit to which has one pass from the grandiose basalt rocks to the gossamer subtleties of the bobbin-lace work, a tradition that is as alive as the pilgrimages to the black Virgin.

Further south, in the Cévennes, the geology of the Massif Central connects again with the Hercynian plateau of its early origins. This overwhelming and austere rampart, looming high above Languedoc, gave birth to a special race of people, the Cévenols, who, generation after generation, made terraces for their cultivation and who became Camisards in order to defend their ideals. Today, these people of the Cévennes are open to tourism – for skiing in winter and hiking or walking in the summer –, but the pastoral activities have survived the rural exodus. The same thing is true for the neighbouring Causses, vast limestone plateaus that resemble steppes, cut through by spectacular gorges such as that of the Tarn and the Jonte. For almost as long as can be remembered, the sheep here are the source of Roquefort cheese, while their lambs have made of Millau one of the capitals of the glove-making industry.

Above: Lacemaker of the puy.
Opposite: Cévennes landscape.
Below: Transhumance in the mountains of Bouge.
Right page: The hamlet of Sainte Enimie in the gorges of the Tarn.

CAMARGUE

Black bulls, white horses, and pink flamingoes are the great personalities of the wild Camargue, the Camargue one thinks of first, this Rhône delta that has the advantages of the protection of a natural park. Next come to mind the images of bullfight festivals in Arles or of parades of herdsmen carrying their tridents like banners, images that have the face of Mireille or the colours of a Van Gogh canvas. For the Camargue also means people proud of their roots, their rich history and lively traditions. Lastly, visions of Sainte-Marie-de-la-Mer come forward, with its church in the sun, two steps away from the waves, a spot that is sacred to the people of Provence, but even more so to gypsies from all over the world.

The "Boumians" converge at the Ca-margue and at this sanctuary in order to venerate the relics of Sarah, their patron saint. The legend tells that it was indeed Saint Marie-Jacobé, the Virgin's sister, and Saint Marie-Salome, mother of two of the apostles, who were thrown onto these shores, after having been chased out of Judea in a small boat without oars or a sail, and were welcomed here by Sarah who was the head of a tribe of gypsies. Thereafter the three women stayed here, near an altar built in thanksgiving, to which the present fortified church, built in the fifteenth century, is heir. On the initiative of King René, excavations then allowed for the discovery of the relics of the saints, which had been hidden during the invasions of the Barbarians, and this is the origin of one of the most consistently sustained and most spectacular pilgrimages of our time.

Saintes-Marie-de-la-Mer:

Upper left: Bulls and cowherd.

Lower left: Pink flamingoes.

Above: Horses and cowherd.

Opposite: The city.

Upper: Avignon.

Above: Vineyard in Baux de Provence.

Centre right page: Landscape in the neighbourhood of Baux de Provence.

Lower right page: Palace of the Popes in Avignon.

PROVENCE

Under a sky whose light never ceases to inspire painters and photographers, Provence unfolds contrasting landscapes, soothing and serene in one place, while elsewhere it is cut out of limestone like so many Dantean sculptures, but always in inimitable harmony. Since time immemorial, humankind seems to have made itself the accomplice of this Provence, although it knew its generosity to be far smaller than its smile. Architectural treasures left behind by the Romans near waterways, feudal sentinels and villages perched high on every peak, olive-groves, vineyards, and fields of lavender as soon as the soil allows it, while rocks, bush or scrubland with aromatic herbs divide up the rest, such is the usual inventory of the land of Provence.

Among the famous sites of Provence, Les Baux holds a special place. Nature has presented this village with an exceptional framework on the edge of the Alpilles mountain chain, history made it the fiefdom of legendary lords, and tradition continues one of the most moving ceremonies one could attend, the midnight mass of the shepherds at Christmas.

More than a lofty place, Avignon by itself is an entire chapter of history, that of the papacy outside of Rome. Since the time that it was the capital of Christianity, the city has maintained a Palace of the Popes, impressive in its power and majesty, as well as a pronounced taste for every form of culture. Innumerable museums, the imprint of Frédéric Mistral, and a stimulating festival are there to prove it.

COTE D'AZUR, CORSICA

Is the Côte d'Azur France's earthly paradise? One would believe so, were one to judge by the number of those who have made themselves a place in the sun there, without even speaking of the mass of summer visitors. And yet, despite the ever-increasing number of resorts and ports of pleasure, this coast remains a marvel. In spite of the traffic jams on the highways that lead there, Saint-Tropez still is the old village of pirates, seafarers, and fishermen, the charm of which was ingeniously immortalized on canvas by Signac, Dufy, Matisse, and ever so many more. Similarly, Menton with its gentle climate and its pictoresque old town has learned how not to sell its soul to tourism, at least no more than it did during the Belle Époque, when it saw its calling as a seaside resort come to life.

Far off in the sea, Corsica is a whole different universe. It is not enough to call it an island, for more than anything else it is a mountain in the sea, showing snowy peaks even in the heat of summer. Besides, Corsicans are much more mountain people than they are seamen, and they remember that for a long time the sea brought them nothing but misfortune in the form of plunderers from the Barbary Coast and elsewhere. Hence the watchtowers on the least little knoll on the shore and those villages that are hidden from view on the steep slopes. Hence the citadels which defy any attack, such as the one of Bonifacio. The site of this city, which links sheer cliffs with a remarkably protected rocky inlet, was actually at the origin of a of a role reversal, since its inhabitants lived off piracy for a long time...

Upper: Tower with eaves of three rows of tiles in Porto.
Above left: The harbour at Saint-Tropez.
Above right: The city of Menton.
Right page: Cliffs of Bonifacio.

THE SOUTHERN ALPS

On the program of the Southern Alps are sunshine and the joy of living, and from this point of view they appear to be an extension of Provence and the Côte d'Azur. Badly hurt by the rural exodus, this region is gaining a new life in our era of diehard leisure seekers. In two decades, summer tourism, hiking, mountain climbing, gliding, bathing in hot springs, sailing – on the reservoirs of dams – , mountainbiking and winter sports have made the Southern Alps and Alpine forelands into an immense terrrain of pleasure and relaxation.

Invigorated, the old towns are cultivating their picturesque qualities, in the manner of Moustiers-Sainte-Marie, Entrevaux or Colmars, while the great natural sites sometimes see their increased number of visitors rival that of the Côte d'Azur. It happens that this is the case for some belvederes of the gorges of the

Above: Cave engravings in the Vallée des Merveilles.
Opposite: The Vallée de Fontgillarde in Queyras.
Upper right: The Vallée de Clausis in Queyras.
Center right: Lavender fields in the neighbourhood of Moustiers-Sainte-Marie.

Verdon, but the enormous size of this famous canyon more often than not allows it to welcome its crowd of admirers. Close to the Italian border, in Mercantour, the Vallée des Merveilles is not so readily approachable; discovering the mysterious hidden carvings means taking an excursion of several hours.

Until quite recently, Queyras, a bit farther north, was not even accessible all year long. Thus, in this region, which is the highest of the continent to have a permanent population, original life styles have developed, human riches preserved by a regional natural park as well as by the Queyras landscapes.

DAUPHINÉ

A bit more restrained than the province from which it took its name, geographical Dauphiné covers the central part of the Alps and the French Alpine foreland, between the Italian border and the banks of the Rhône. Four entities can be distinguished here; first the central massifs, Queyras, Oisans, and Belledonne, the universe of eternal snow; the Alpine pass in which Grenoble lies between Grésivaudan and the region of Drac; the Alpine forelands, of which Vercors and Chartreuse are the bastions; and finally lower Dauphiné, a region of hills in which tobacco and vineyards in particular, profit much from the sunshine.

However, many people see the Alps primarily through names such as Val-d'Isère, Courchevel, or those of other resorts of the Vannoise massif, which have recently been host to the trials of the Olympic Games. To this skiing paradise some people prefer the land of plenty of the high altitudes found in the Écrins, a massif of harsh grandeur that stretches between Meije and Pelvoux in the eastern part of Oisans. Still others do no more than watch the snow and rocks from a distance, but on the other hand have a great interest in studying the fauna and flora of the high mountain pastures close-up, a fascinating spectacle in the summer months. Frequently these visistors also take time to appreciate the manner in which people have succeeded in leading their life at such heights, notably by building homes of wood and flat stone which seem to form one with their environment.

Opposite: The Village of La Grave
and the glacier of Meije.

SAVOIE

The landscapes of the Savoie call for every superlative in the book, grandiose as for example with the Horseshoe of Sixt or the Sea of Ice, romantic as the Lac du Bourget, forever associated with the name of Lamartine, or transformed into stadiums of snow as may be seen at Mégève, Morzine or La Cluzaz. On the crossroads between France, Italy, and Switzerland, Chamonix stands as the capital of these triumphant Alps, being both a summer holiday centre and a skiing and mountain climbing resort of the highest order. From the depth of the valley of Chamonix and from the city's centre itself, people practicing the most varied forms of ascent depart to assault the heights, and even the least athletic tourist can enjoy the most dizzying look-out points. Everything is possible, from

Upper: Aerial view of the sea of ice.
Above: The Alps in the fall and the
Mont-Blanc.
Center right: Horseshoe of Samoëns.
Lower right: Ski resort of Cluzaz.

the ever valiant little train of Montenvers to the ski-lifts of the peak of the Midi and the Vallée Blanche, in the trail of Monsieur Dumollet as much as in that of mountain climbing pioneers, whose exploits can be remembered in the course of a complete crossing of the massif of the Mont-Blanc into Italy.

The edges of the Mont-Blanc, and up to a point its summit, have become so democratized that one tends to forget they once played the now forgotten role of the Everest. For a long time these hellish areas were not known, then people began to measure their full height from below. Finally, on the 8th of August, 1786, accompanied by Paccard and Balmat from Chamonix, Bénédict de Saussure from Geneva, opened the era of mountain climbing when he reached the rooftop of Europe at 4807 metres.

THE RHONE VALLEY

A road of passage since the beginning of time, but an ill-defined regional entity, the Rhône Valley encroaches upon very diverse areas. Lower Dauphiné and Tricastin on the left bank thus face Vivarais and Ardèche, regions that have nothing in common other than that they give their waterways to the Rhône and their wines to French gastronomy.

The Rhône Valley happily alternates monuments and natural points of interest and among the former there is the Château de Grignan which occupies a place of honour in that it marks the great door to Provence. This sumptuous Renaissance home, built by Count François de Grignan, Louis XIV's lieutenant-general in Provence, owes part of its fame to the Marquise the Sévigné, whose daughter De Grignan had married.

The epistolary author spent long periods of time at Grignan, and it is there, under the Tricastin sun, that she died in 1696.

As for the natural riches, the right bank of the Rhône has been favoured, with the reliefs through which the Ardèche has forced itself a spectacular passage. Lovers of canoeing and kayaking come by the thousands every year and are in ecstasy before the impressive settings of the gorges of this turbulent river. The great moment of the descent is of course the one where one passes underneath the natural arch of the Pont d'Arc. The limestone plateaus are not to be outdone and well worth a look, for here several abysses of remarkable concretions can be seen, among which the extraordinary swallow hole of Orgnac.

Left page: Façade of the Château de Grignan.
Above: Swallow hole of Orgnac.
Opposite: The Château de Grignan.

LYON AND REGION

The capital of the Rhône-Alpes region, an industrious city on the crossroads and a metropolis animated by European ambitions, Lyon does not enjoy the reputation that its importance would imply. It is true that the city does not give easily of itself, but what greater pleasure for the visitor who takes the time to discover its many attractions! Around the masterful Place Bellecour, which marks its centre, Lyon is in fact composed of a juxtaposition of districts, the landmarks of which are the Saône and the Rhône on one side, and two hills on the other, Fourvière and Croix-Rousse. According to the famous saying of Michelet, the former, with its convents and basilica, is where one prays, while the second one, with its silk-workers and narrow alleys belongs to the labourers. At the foot of Fourvière around the cathedral, the quarter of Saint-Jean is just as remarkable with the most extensive complex of French Renaissance architecture. In short, from traffic jam to museum – the city has twenty-four of them – from the Roman amphitheatre to the new Opera, Lyon is rich and pleasant enough to hold the attention of its guests for several days, all things considered.

Picturesque Vieux Lyon and its wonderful gastronomic surprises are an invitation to walk a little farther, toward the great tourist spots. Near the Dombes, for example, it is essential to see at least Pérouges, with its extraordinary medieval setting, and the church of Brou, built in the sixteenth century by Marguerite of Austria, at the Portes de la Bresse.

*Upper: Lyon: The quays of the Saône
and the Fourvière hill.*

*Above: The church of Brou in Bourg-
en-Bresse.*

BOURGOGNE

Known worldwide for its wines, its cuisine, and its artistic treasures, Bourgogne (Burgundy) has paradoxically remained off the beaten track from the great tourist routes. Several approaches might guide a visit to this province, of which the vineyard, that comes to mind immediately, is not by any means the least interesting one. The entire history of Bourgogne refers to it, with the grapeseeds that were found in the prehistoric vestiges of the rock of Solutré – today Pouilly-Fuissé is produced there – then the first vines planted by the Gallo-Romans. This was followed by the vineyard labour of the monks of Citeaux, and finally by the sales venture undertaken by the great dukes of the West who proudly proclaimed themselves the "lords of the best wines in all of Christendom". Dijon, the ancient and magnificent capital of these princes who competed with the kings of France, is similarly surrounded by prestigious towns that were like so many diamonds in their crown. Of these, the most lustrous one is Beaune, where the dukes had settled before they went to Dijon. The hospices of the town, a true Gothic palace filled with works of art, serve each year as the setting for the most famous auction of the great wines. The Burgundian vineyards owe much to the monastic orders, especially to the monks of Cluny, who perfected the method of dressing the vine, known as "la taille courte"; but for this monastic order the essence lay in spirituality and it was this that allowed the order to spread its influence across the continent. Its symbol is the "mother" abbey, whose church at the height of its splendour surpassed even Saint Peter's in Rome in its gigantic size.

Above: Cluny.
Centre left, right page: Detail of the Cour d'Honneur of the hospices in Beaune.
Centre right, right page: Detail of a house on Rue Suzon in Dijon.
Lower right page: The Abbey of Cluny.

FRANCHE-COMTÉ

Often linked with Bourgogne, with which it shares certain traits such as the multi-coloured tiles of some of its belltowers, Franche-Comté is endowed with a personality all its own. For the province, reigned over by Besançon, is essentially that of the Jura, that is to say of trout rivers, gorges, and waterfalls, cliffs pierced through with caves, abbeys hidden in the depth of forests, and pasture-lands full of Montbéliard cows from whom come some of the most superb cheeses. A similar reputation is associated with the cold meats of the Jura, as well as with the wine of Ardois which comes from the foothills of the mountain.

This is also the Franche-Comté of meticulous crafts, developed to make the best of the long winter's isolation. Watchmaking, the making of eyeglasses, and woodworking are local specialties, from which a unique tradition emerges, that of the production of pipes in Saint-Claude. This industry, which appeared a hundred and fifty years ago when the root of Corsican briar was introduced into the region, quickly took over from the production of crucifixes and other rosaries, which until then were the prerogative of the local craftspeople. Before mass production caused this activity to decrease, Saint-Claude had, in fact, become the world capital of the briar pipe. The high qualification of the people of Franche-Comté has also put them in a choice place when it comes to the cutting of diamonds and gemstones, work that is the focus of an exhibition near the original Gothic cathedral of Saint-Claude.

Left page: The Saint-Jean Cathedral in Besançon.

Upper: Manufacturing pipes in Saint-Claude.
Above left: School for dairy industrie in Poligny.
Above right: Traditional cold meat shop.
Overleaf: The village of Grandfontaine in the Massif du Donon.

93

VOSGES, ALSACE

In the north-east corner of France, the crests of the Vosges line themselves up like a frontier between the Alsatians and the "interior people", as they call their compatriots. On these mountains and in the plains of Alsace, all along the Rhine, Alsatian is in fact the spoken language, and the visitor is reminded of this every second, from signposts to wrought iron shop signs or from winelabel to cookbook recipe. This land remains foreign for only a moment, for few of the provinces have such a knack for welcoming their visitors. Everything breathes spiritedness, joviality, and love of beautiful things, in the image of villages that could not be dreamed of as more colourful, flowered, and exuberant, especially in the wine-growing south and around Colmar. At the other end of Alsace, Stras-bourg sits enthroned, the European calling of which is well-matched with its origin as the "city of roads", at the crossroads of the land- and waterways of the continent. Surpassing the city's rooftops in its height, the Notre-Dame Cathedral also symbolized this calling, having been built by architects and sculptors from both sides of the Rhine. Similarly, Goethe came to Strasbourg to look for the tomb of Erwin de Steinbach, the foreman of the façade, thereby preceding Victor Hugo who wanted to climb the highest Gothic spire in existence. His notes describe an "old city with notched gables and with large roofs with skylights, intersected by towers and churches." And again "the Ill and the Rhine, two pretty rivers which brighten this dark mass of buildings with their pools of bright and green water".

Left page: View of Strasbourg.
Above: The Notre-Dame cathedral in Strasbourg.
Opposite: The Pass of Charbonnière.

LORRAINE

With Nancy and Metz, Lorraine is in the possession of two capitals. Lunéville is the Versailles of this province, since Stanislas, the king of Poland, moved his court there, while Toul is its sacred city, built around an extraordinary cathedral, Saint-Étienne, which is a jewel of the high Gothic period. As one passes through Lorraine, one can still see the land of Joan the Maiden, with Domrémy, and further down, on the Meuse, there is Verdun, the theatre of one of the greatest exploits of the "poilus" (the hairy ones), as the French soldiers were called during W.W. I. Four hundred thousand of them, among whom the famous Unknown Soldier, fell in battle so that the town would survive. This is to say that many a major chapter of French history was written in these regions.

But not everything was a battle. Pépin le Bref and Charlemagne used to love staying in Lorraine at a time when Metz and Verdun were already appreciated centres of culture. The era of the dukes, despite many vicissitudes, brought the province a lasting prosperity which went accompanied by a remarkable artistic flourishing, especially during the sixteenth and seventeenth centuries: the name of the painter Le Lorrain alone is enough to give an indication of this. During the Age of Enlightenment, Lorraine came to know the princely splendours that decorated Nancy with exceptional monuments, and this creative period was prolonged to a certain extent in the famous School of Nancy at the end of the last century.

Opposite: The Hôtel de Ville in Toul.

*Above: Vineyards in the
neighbourhood of Cramant.
Opposite: The apse of the Notre-
Dame cathedral in Reims.
Right: Fortified castle in Sedan.*

CHAMPAGNE, ARDENNE

Champagne! In every language of the world it is a synonym for celebration, whether that be an athletic victory, the lauching of a ship, a great formal wedding or an intimate evening of lovers. In France, however, the name of the famous sparkling wine has not made people forget the province to which it is linked, Champagne, just as fertile in medieval masterpieces, this province of which Troyes and Reims are the other emblems. Having entered history with the baptism of Clovis by Saint Rémi, in 498, Reims then became the city of coronations. Twenty-five kings knelt down for this ceremony, among whom Charles VII in the presence of Joan of Arc, in 1429. These great moments took place, of course, in the Notre-Dame Cathedral, the gem of decorated Gothic architecture, which chronologically came after Chartres. On the outside, special notice should be taken of the western façade, admirable in its proportions and vertical thrust; and among the rich statuary of the thirteenth century that frames the portals, of the smiling Angel, which deservedly appears as one of the high points of medieval sculpture. The interior of Notre-Dame de Reims is not any less effective, with the other side of the façade also decorated with innumerable statues and lit by two rose windows that become magnificent at dusk.

In Champagne, several fortresses stood like sentinels on the road of the invasions, but the first line of defense, meant to preserve Paris, was in Ardenne, with Rocroi, Charleville-Mézières, and Sedan, where the fifteenth century château, connected to the name Turenne, is the most extensive one in Europe.

FRANCE IMERSION CPL (MINERVA) Sig. 6 Nois

ILE-DE-FRANCE

Originally, Ile-de-France was nothing more than a minuscule plain north of Paris and it is not known how the name has come to designate a vast region the heart of which is Paris. The presence of the City of Lights leaves Ile-de-France in the shadows; many visitors know it only for the Château de Versailles and EuroDisney. For someone willing to take the time to know it more closely, the region begins by revealing the wealth of its landscapes, which offer many harmonious variations on the themes of agricultural plateaus, royal forests, and green flowing valleys. To these may be added the multitude of small regions that make Ile-de-France into a mosaic illustrating a great many aspects of the French genius: the Plaine de France, Parisis, Goële, Valois, Senlisis, French Vexin, Mantois, Hurepoix, Yvelines, Brie, Gâtinais, and Beauce. Just to mention the great monuments alone, Ile-de-France reads like a catalogue of royal châteaux, from Dourdan, the oldest one of which only traces remain, to those that illustrate the pinnacle of the Ancien Régime and even the Empire with Malmaison. And if they did not belong directly to a sovereign ruler, such as Vaux-le-Vicomte, built by Nicolas Fouquet, these châteaux all had their place in history. Fontainebleau, Chantilly, and at the gates of the capital, Vincennes, Saint-Germain-en-Laye, and Versailles, so many châteaux that speak better than any book of the Middle Ages, the Renaissance, and the Golden Age, whether the subject be architecture, the artistic heritage, or the art of landscaping gardens.

Above: The Château de Versailles.
Centre right:
Château de Vaux-le-Vicomte.
Lower right: Château de Chantilly.

PARIS

It has often been said that the twenty centuries of the history of France were not any longer than the Seine River between Ile-Saint-Louis and the Pont de la Concorde. Today this should probably be pushed all the way to the bottom of the towers of the Défense so as to account for the end of the current millenium, but it is true that Paris is more than just the capital of France. The city contains the roots of the country, the French spirit blows over it, and the ambitions of Paris are the ambitions of the nation.

One of the obligatory stops in the discovery of Paris is the top of the Eiffel Tower, a monument of iron constructed on the occasion of the Revolution's centenary. From up there, to quote Giraudoux, one's gaze kisses "the hundred thousand hectares in the world where the most thinking, speaking, and writing has been done". From the dome of the Sacré-Coeur of Montmartre, consecrated after the 1918 victory, the view is no less attractive and extends for a radius of 50 kilometres around. The belltower of the basilica holds one of the largest church bells known, the Savoyarde, which weighs almost 20 tons.

In its image, Paris is a city of superlatives. The Arc de Triomphe is the largest in the world, Garnier's Opera also held the record for its genre, the Place de la Concorde is one of the most impressive squares in existence, the Louvre and its museum have no equal elsewhere, and all else is in keeping. Weary of these kinds of feats, one can explore a more intimist Paris, that of the booksellers, the restaurants, the small boutiques that make the eyes of foreigners shine, the cabarets or the Jardin des Plantes.

Upper: Paris Metro station.
Above left: Paris: The Sacré-Coeur in Montmartre.
Above right: Paris: The Place de la Concorde.
Right: The Eiffel Tower.

PARIS

Medieval Paris, having grown in a disorderly fashion where, for example, the houses almost mounted an attack on the Notre-Dame, disappeared in the nineteenth century under the aegis of Baron Haussmann. Today's capital is still, to a great extent, the heir of this urban designer's views, recently served by a cleaning of all the ancient monuments and of the façades that stand along most of the boulevards. But Paris, always in touch with its era, could not leave it at that.

Sometimes stirring up the people's excitability, but affirming the role Paris plays in France and in the world, a series of important construction projects in these last few years are in the process of giving buildings of a daring architecture that are much in the spirit of the times to the capital city. In particular, these are the Centre Pompidou in Beaubourg, the Institut du Monde Arabe, the Opera de la Bstille, the Palais Omnisports in Bercy, the Ministry of Finances, and the Grande Bibliothèque.

The most spectacular of this contemporary flowering stand along the triumphal way, dreamed of by Colbert, beginning at the Louvre, and extended in our time to the Défense. This masteful axis thus begins with the renovation of the Grand Louvre and the famous glass Pyramid designed by the Chinese architect, Ieoh Ming Pei, passes by the Tuileries and the Champs-Elysées, and departs towards infinity across the perspective of a startling Grande Arche, created by a Dane. More than ever enamoured of the universal and the cultural, the City of Lights has certainly not lost its soul.

Above: The Opera de la Bastille.
Center right: Paris: View of the Seine and bridges.
Lower right: Paris: The Pyramid of the Louvre.

TABLE OF CONTENTS

INDEX OF NAMES CITED

PHOTO CREDITS